TRY IT! BUY IT!

VINTAGE ADVERTS

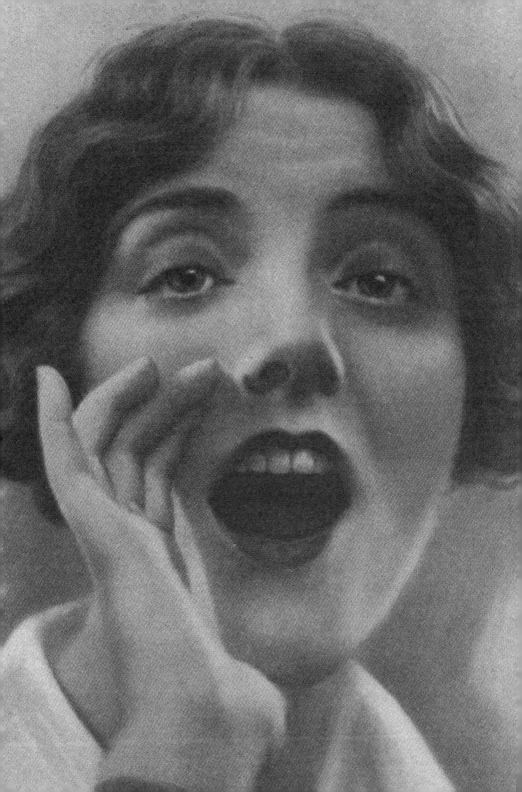

TRY IT! BUY IT!

VINTAGE ADVERTS

BRITISH LIBRARY

First published in 2015 by
The British Library
96 Euston Road
London NW1 2DB

British Library Cataloguing in Publication Data
A catalogue record for this book is available
from the British Library

ISBN 978 0 7123 5758 6

Designed by Rawshock Design
Picture research by Sally Nicholls
Printed in Malta by Gutenberg Press

INTRODUCTION

The man who first took advantage of the general curiosity that was excited by a siege of a battle to betray the readers of news into the knowledge of the shop where the best puffs and powders were to be sold was undoubtedly a man of great sagacity, and profound skill in the nature of man. But when he had once shown the way it was easy to follow him.

SAMUEL JOHNSON, 'THE ART OF ADVERTISING EXEMPLIFIED',
FROM *THE IDLER*, 20 JANUARY 1759

Advertising is not new. It is evident right from the birth of printing. One of the earliest known printed advertisements is a handbill printed by Caxton in 1477 for the 'Pyes of Salisbury'. Pyes were clerical rules, in this instance setting out the method by which the clergy in Salisbury dealt with the changing date of Easter.

A notice for the recovery of twelve stolen horses – published in the *Kingdom's Weekly Intelligencer* in 1647 – is often quoted as the first newspaper advertisement. One of the advantages of a printed newspaper advert, as opposed to a handbill, was that the newspapers were distributed to and kept by the coffeehouses, booksellers and inns of the time. Within these establishments they were perused by many, rather than being thrown away unread as was the case with many handbills. Patent medicines were a frequent subject of such notices. Quack doctors were in many ways the pioneers of modern marketing, branding their products and advertising them widely over large areas of the country.

The eighteenth century saw the proliferation of newspapers, and considerable thought was put into the writing and presentation of advertisements. Joseph Addison writing in *The Tatler* in 1712 commented: 'The great art of writing advertisements is the finding out a proper method to catch the reader's eye, without which a good thing may pass unobserved...But the great skill in an advertiser is seen chiefly in the style which he makes use of. He is to mention the Universal Esteem, or General Reputation of things that were never heard of.'

William Taylor is acknowledged to have established the first advertising agency in 1786. He contracted himself to the newspapers to fill blank space and essentially just passed on to the papers copy written by the advertiser, rather than writing his own.

By 1800, James White, who founded an agency in London, seems to have written copy himself for different advertisers and to have employed his friend, the essayist Charles Lamb, as a copywriter. With the emergence of advertising agencies, advertising became an institution, which employed many aspiring novelists and journalists as copywriters.

The nineteenth century saw three developments that led to a proliferation of adverts in the form that we recognise today. The first was the development of modern printing methods: the mechanised printing press, stereotyping and the introduction of colour lithographic processes. The second was the abolishment of newspaper and advertising stamp duty, which led to an explosion in newspapers and periodicals loaded with increasingly illustrated adverts. The third was the development of manufacturing and the proliferation of mass-produced items. No longer were the shops full of local hand-made goods; instead factory-made products from all over the country and abroad came to dominate. Such goods sought markets a long way from the factories, sometimes on the other side of the world. Consumer goods advertising grew rapidly, and clever packaging and branding were now necessary to their success. Henry Sampson in his *History of Advertising* (1874) encapsulated this trend by declaring that 'the essence of advertising is to place your statement where it is most likely to be seen by those most interested in it'.

Thomas J. Barrett of Pears soap is sometimes called the 'father of advertising' for his pioneering ad campaign, which used targeted slogans and immediately recognisable images. Barrett bought the copyright to John Everett Millais' painting *Bubbles*, added a bar of Pears soap to the image, and created one of the most famous adverts in history. Pears soap was the world's first legally registered brand, but others soon followed and developed their own slogan- and image-led advertising campaigns. Many of the most iconic late nineteenth-century adverts are for brands that are still going strong today.

Mass marketing continued to expand into the twentieth century, with the major growth area being repeat-purchase consumer goods. The development of psychological science, well established by 1914, led to cleverly targeted slogans. Women in particular were the targets for household purchasing. The introduction of 'hire-purchase' agreements also spurred the advertisements for big-ticket items such as cars, refrigerators and vacuum cleaners. The First World War saw few adverts for luxury goods but fierce competition between cigarette brands, and many patriotic appeals to consumers, while the inter-war period saw the triumph of colour advertising in periodicals and was a time of expansion. It was a golden age of advertising.

The British Library's collections of ephemera, in the Evanion Collection, and its unrivalled collection of newspapers and magazines, provides a rich resource to exploit for vivid, tempting, intriguing and amusing early advertisements.

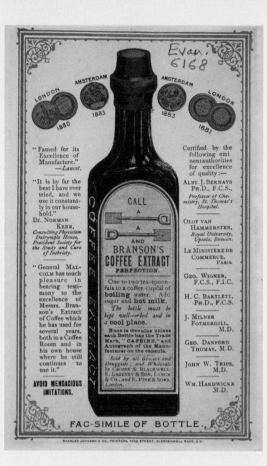

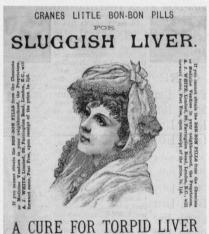

OPPOSITE: Gulliver's Whisky Curacoa, *c.* 1883.

TOP LEFT: 'Call a Spade a Spade'. Branson's Coffee Extract, *c.* 1885. The advert includes press testimonials arranged around the central illustration.

BOTTOM LEFT: 'A cure for torpid liver and a beautifier of the complexion'. Cranes Little Bon-Bon Pills for sluggish liver, *c.* 1885.

Fac-Simile of Bottle.

Bvan. 5192.

CHA^s. BAKER & C^{o's}. STORES

Dec. 1883.

BOYS' CLOTHING AT TRADE PRICE

YOUTHS' SUITS	KILT SUITS	SULTAN SUITS	CAPE OVERCOATS	NORFOLK SUITS	OVERCOATS	JERSEY SUITS	YOUTH'S MORNING COAT. AND VEST
8/11 10/9	5/11	2/11 3/11	5/11 8/11	8/11	3/11 4/11	5/11 to 8/11	24/6 29/6 34/6
12/11 16/11	8/11 10/9	5/11	12/11 16/11	10/9 12/11	8/11 8/11	according to size.	
19/11	14/11	8/11 12/11		16/11	10/9 14/11		

~∞≈ NEW DEPARTMENTS ARE NOW OPEN FOR ≈∞~

HOSIERY, SHIRTS, HATS, BOOTS, SHOES, &c.

— AT CIVIL SERVICE STORE PRICES. —

ETON SUITS	RUGBY SUITS	YOUTHS' OVERCOATS	SAILOR SUITS	MAN-OF-WAR SUITS	NAP REEFERS	LADIES' ULSTERS
34/6 39/6	9/11 12/11	12/11 16/11	3/6 4/11	9/11 12/11	8/11 to 14/11	To measure,
To Order,	16/11 19/11	19/11 24/6	6/11 8/11	18/11	According to size.	39/6 44/6 49/6
42/6 49/6						Other styles,
						29/6 39/6

BOYS' SCHOOL OUTFITS.
25 PER CENT UNDER USUAL PRICES

CITY BRANCH, 82, FLEET STREET.	HEAD DEPOT 271 & 272, HIGH HOLBORN.	NEW BRANCH 137 & 138, TOTTENHAM COURT R^D.

NEW ILLUSTRATED PRICE LISTS WITH PATTERNS OF CLOTH AND SELF MEASUREMENT FORMS SENT POST FREE ON APPLICATION AT HEAD DEPOT.

CARRIAGE PAID TO ANY RAILWAY STATION IN ENGLAND, IRELAND OR SCOTLAND.

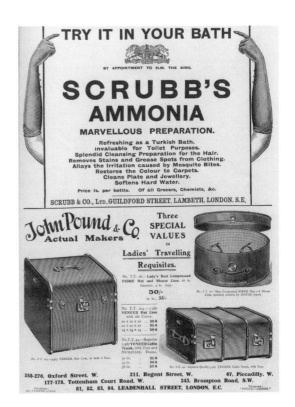

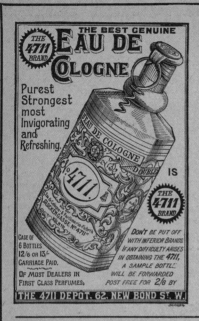

14

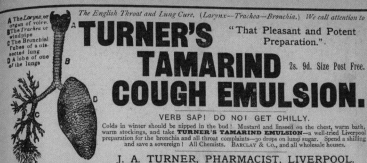

The English Throat and Lung Cure. *(Larynx—Trachea—Bronchia.) We call attention to*

TURNER'S

TAMARIND

COUGH EMULSION.

"That Pleasant and Potent Preparation."

2s. 9d. Size Post Free.

A The *Larynx*, or organ of voice.
B The *Trachea* or windpipe
C The Bronchial Tubes of a dissected lung
D A lobe of one of the lungs

VERB SAP! DO NOT GET CHILLY.

Colds in winter should be nipped in the bud! Mustard and linseed on the chest, warm bath, warm stockings, and take **TURNER'S TAMARIND EMULSION**—a well-tried Liverpool preparation for the bronchia and all throat complaints—30 drops on lump sugar. Spend a shilling and save a sovereign! All Chemists. BARCLAY & Co., and all wholesale houses.

J. A. TURNER, PHARMACIST, LIVERPOOL.

THE ORIGINAL.

JEWSBURY & BROWN'S

THE ORIGINAL.

WHITE SOUND TEETH.

FRAGRANT BREATH.

HEALTHY GUMS.

Used in all Countries for
OVER 70 YEARS.

CAUTION.—Beware of Counterfeits. The only Genuine is signed "JEWSBURY & BROWN."

ORIENTAL TOOTH PASTE

WORTH A GUINEA A BOX.

BEECHAM'S

PILLS.

THE SALE IS NOW
SIX MILLION BOXES
PER ANNUM.

FOR ALL

Bilious and Nervous Disorders, such as

Sick Headache, Constipation,

Weak Stomach, Impaired Digestion,

Disordered Liver and Female Ailments.

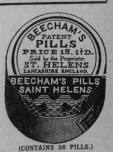

PREPARED ONLY BY THE PROPRIETOR—

THOMAS BEECHAM, ST. HELENS, LANCASHIRE.

Sold by all Druggists and Patent Medicine Dealers everywhere, in Boxes, at 9½d., 1s. 1½d., and 2s. 9d. each. Full Directions with each Box.

(CONTAINS 56 PILLS.)

OPPOSITE AND ABOVE:
Assorted adverts, showing different
typographical approaches, from
Scribner's magazine, 1905.

J. B. B

PRAC...

BELL HANGE

AND GAS

193, LOWE

DE

WORK DONE BY CO...

BOTTLE JACKS & MODERAT...

Evan. 9046

ILES,

ICAL

LOCKSMITH,

FITTER,

STREET,

L.

ACT OR OTHERWISE.

LAMPS CLEANED & REPAIRED.

P.T.O.

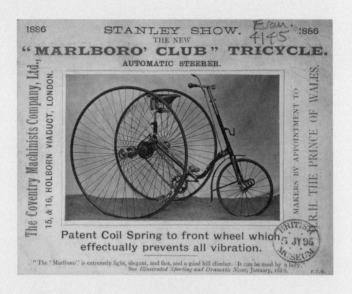

1886 STANLEY SHOW. 1886
THE NEW
"MARLBORO' CLUB" TRICYCLE.
AUTOMATIC STEERER.

Patent Coil Spring to front wheel which
effectually prevents all vibration.

"The 'Marlboro' is extremely light, elegant, and fast, and a good hill climber. It can be used by a lady.
See *Illustrated Sporting and Dramatic News*, January, 1886.

Some Cyclists

know the *real* joy and pleasure
of cycling—that is to say, those
who ride the

RALEIGH

the all-steel bicycle

get the *full* enjoyment out of
cycling. Raleighs are fitted with
Brooks Saddle, Dunlop Tyres,
Sturmey-Archer 3-speed Gear,
and the best of everything.
Send to-day for illustrated
"Book of the Raleigh," free.

Raleigh Cycle Co., Nottingham
AGENTS EVERYWHERE.

ABOVE: 'It can be used by a lady'.
Trade card for The new 'Marlboro'
Club' tricycle, The Coventry
Machinists Company, 1886.

LEFT AND OPPOSITE: It was not
just periodicals and newspapers
that ran advertisements. Many
book publishers also relied on
advertising revenue, making
available the inside front and
back pages. Here, rival bicycle
companies from inside *Some
Cyclists - not forgetting the aunts*
by the Owl, 1912.

TRIUMPH

CYCLING on a TRIUMPH is what makes this pastime fascinating, easy and health giving.

When you buy a TRIUMPH you can always reckon on it giving you good service, such great care is taken in the workmanship, in the selection of material, and—

There is really no necessity to purchase an unknown and un-branded machine on the score of price, as TRIUMPHS are but little more expensive and will outlast any cheaply constructed bicycle by many thousands of miles.

Prices from £6 17s. 6d. to £12

TRIUMPH CYCLE CO., Ltd., Coventry.

London—4-5, Holborn Viaduct, E.C.   Leeds—4, King Edward St. Manchester—160, Deansgate. Glasgow—14, Waterloo St.

AGENTS EVERYWHERE.

ABOVE: Adverts from *Scribner's Magazine*, 1905.

OPPOSITE: Beecham's Pills advert from *Illustrated Sporting and Dramatic News*, 1898.

20

OPPOSITE: Sunlight soap poster,
c. 1900. Sunlight Soap became
the world's first packaged, branded,
laundry soap in 1886.

ABOVE: Lifebuoy soap, battling
against the stormy seas of dirt
and disease c. 1900. The image
references Grace Darling, a
lighthouse keeper's daughter
famed for rescuing survivors of
a shipreck in 1838.

SMART CUMBERLAND TWEED SUITS
FOR HOLIDAY WEAR AT SPECIAL PRICES.

We are making a speciality of Holiday and Early Autumn Jumper Suits, which are made in our own workrooms during the between seasons, in order to keep our workers fully employed. These garments are well cut and tailored, made from thoroughly reliable materials, and, at the prices marked, are of exceptional value.

Write for Catalogue
of
Smart Knitted
Sports Wear.

SMART HOLIDAY SUIT, plain well-cut skirt in Cumberland Tweed, stockinette jumper trimmed with tweed to match skirt; a most practical and useful garment. In shades of fawn, brown and grey.

Special Price **6½ Gns.**

Stitched Velour Finished Felt Hat to match suit, in many good colourings; various sizes. **29/6.**

PRACTICAL JUMPER SUIT in soft Cumberland Tweed, cut on perfectly tailored lines; attractively trimmed with material in soft colourings to tone; novelty pockets; plain well-cut skirt pleated at one side only. In shades of brown, fawn and grey.

Special Price **7½ Gns.**

Smart Fur Felt Hat to match, in various sizes, and good colourings **49/6.**

USEFUL HOLIDAY SUIT, the skirt in Cumberland Tweed, with deep pleats at side to give ample freedom of movement; stockinette jumper trimmed with tweed to match skirt. In shades of brown, fawn and grey.

Special Price **6½ Gns.**

Stitched Velour Finished Felt Hat to match suit, in various sizes, and many good colourings **29/6.**

DEBENHAM & FREEBODY
(Debenhams Ltd.)

WIGMORE STREET AND WELBECK STREET, LONDON, W.1

ABOVE: Essential country wear,
advertised in *Britannia & Eve*, 1920.

OPPOSITE: Lotus Shoes for
sale in *The Bystander*, 1926.

Lotus are British

Made in Stafford and Northampton and supplied by more than 560 agents in London and the Provinces. Lotus is entirely a British enterprise. Write for Autumn catalogue. Address: LOTUS, STAFFORD.

The makers of Lotus were awarded the Grand Prix at the Brussels Exhibition.

48—13/9

78—17/9

77—13/9

Local agents stock Lotus in numerous sizes and w'dths and give purchasers a first-class fit.

Your local agent can get by return of post any Lotus you prefer if not in his stock—see catalogue.

27—17/9

58—21/-

57—17/9

Wearers of Lotus can always get further pairs like the last. Write for catalogue.

Once fitted, always fitted

A GIRL CAN DRIVE THE

For 7 cwt. loads

£200

COMPLETE

SEE OUR AGENT IN YOUR TOWN

VAN

EASILY & SAFELY

EVERYTHING connected with this light delivery van has been designed to help the driver and to save money for the owner. The control is so simple that the driver has confidence from the start, the brakes acting quickly with smoothness and power and the greatest ease. The 'Overland' Van is easy to start and easy to stop; it costs little to buy and little to maintain. Every point for which the van buyer should look is embodied in the 'Overland': it is the highest yielding investment in the commercial world to-day.

Willys-Overland. Ltd.
151-153 Great Portland Street. London.W.

Telephone:
Mayfair 6700
(5 lines).

Telegrams:
" Wilovelon,
London."

ABOVE: With the men away in the trenches, women were increasingly employed on the home front. *Punch*, 1916.

OPPOSITE: Goodyear footwear, *Footwear Organiser*, 1919.

Cadbury's Cocoa

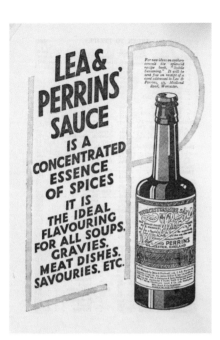

LEFT AND BELOW: Culinary aids, as advertised in the new edition of Mrs Beeton's *Sixpenny Cookery*, 1923.

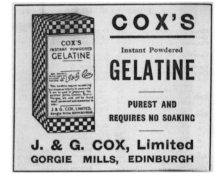

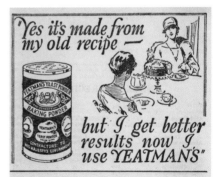

Nobody listens nowadays,
but everybody looks. Say it with a 'Kodak'
snapshot. It speaks so much more
clearly than words.

OPPOSITE: A variation on the adage that a picture speaks louder than words. *Britannia & Eve*, 1929.

LEFT TOP AND BOTTOM: For the most up-to-date cook: an electric cooker, and Nestlé's "Ideal" Milk, both advertised in the new edition of Mrs Beeton's *Sixpenny Cookery*, 1923. "Ideal" Milk is canned evaporated milk and still in production.

ABOVE AND RIGHT: The use of packaging as advertising. Paper bags for a fishmonger, 1885, and an Indian delicatessen, 1886. The latter indicates the growing Indian population in 19th-century London.

OPPOSITE: Pens, linen, bicycles, baby food, razors, cough pills, ice-skating, malt wine and metal polish, all advertised together in *Punch's Alamanck for 1897*.

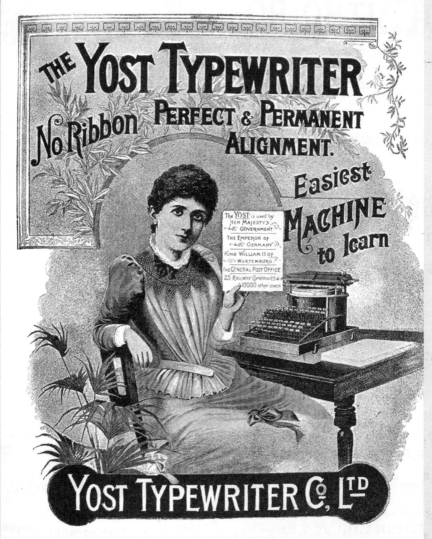

OPPOSITE AND ABOVE: Two new inventions of the 1860s considered suitable for women to use; the Yost Typewriter, in *The British Lithographer*, 1891; and New Rapid Cycles, in *The Gentlewoman*, 1897.

ABOVE: The Victorian woman happy
in her garden. Catalogue for Webb's
Select Seed list, 1885.

OPPOSITE: The sophisticated,
smoking woman of the 1920s.
Player's Navy Cut cigarettes,
The Tatler, 1929.

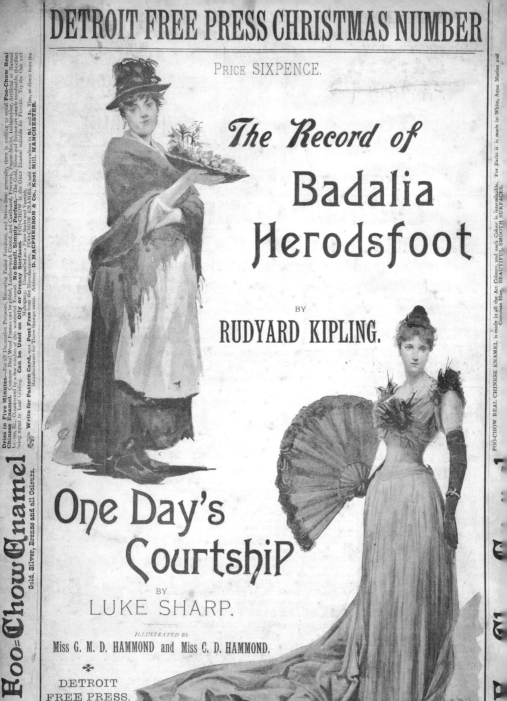

DETROIT FREE PRESS CHRISTMAS NUMBER

PRICE SIXPENCE.

The Record of Badalia Herodsfoot

BY

RUDYARD KIPLING.

One Day's Courtship

BY

LUKE SHARP.

ILLUSTRATED BY

Miss G. M. D. HAMMOND and Miss C. D. HAMMOND.

❖

DETROIT
FREE PRESS,
310, STRAND,
LONDON, W.C.

Rowntree's
PRIZE MEDAL
Rock
Cocoa
CONTAINS ONLY COCOA AND SUGAR

OPPOSITE: Trade card for Rowntree's Rock Cocoa, 1884.

LEFT: The bucolic setting is presumably intended to reinforce the idea of tinned soup as healthy, natural food. *The Tatler*, 1929.

ABOVE LEFT: Trade card for Gordon & Dilworth's Tomato Catsup. The text on the reverse of the card proclaims this is 'The Popular National Sauce of America... Most Delicious! Try it! Buy it!'.

MORE FREE

48

WELCOME

HASKELL ROYAL 2/- EACH

OF ALL DEALERS
AND PROFESSIONALS
OR FROM
THE SOLE MANUFACTURERS
THE **B. F. GOODRICH Co.**
7, SNOW HILL, LONDON, E.C.

A sample ball sent post free on
receipt of P.O. value 2/- from
the manufacturers.

"I must have his name & address- he's driven beyond the limit."

PREVIOUS PAGES: Various culinary
innovations advertised in Mrs
Beeton's *The Book of Household
Management*, 1892.

ABOVE: Haskell Royal Golf Balls,
Golf Illustrated, 1908.

RIGHT: The best of British for those
serving the Raj. Red Ensign Coffee,
The Times of India Annual, 1919.

OPPOSITE: Isle of Man Tourist Board
poster, designed by John Hassal,
1929.

DOUGLAS
ISLE OF MAN
ISLE OF MAN
"It's no tail!"
FOR HAPPY HOLIDAYS

COLMAN'S

MUSTARD

ALL OVER THE WORLD.

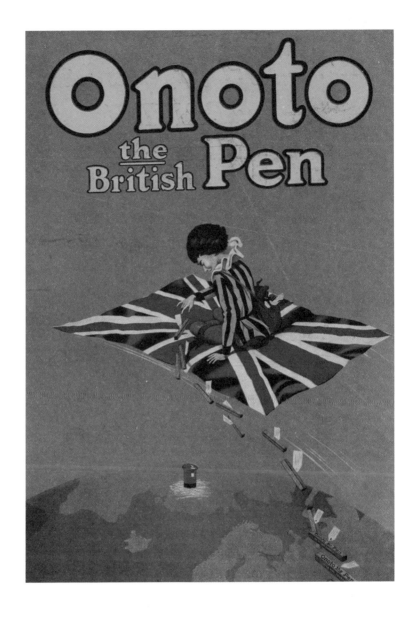

OPPOSITE: The design and
typography make a real attempt
to convey speed. *The Tatler*, 1929.

RIGHT: Trade card for Scott's Cod
Liver Oil, 1884.

A Closed Car of perfect comfort

WITH FOUR WIDE DOORS & FRAMELESS GLASS WINDOWS
The 12/24 h.p.

Lagonda

BRITISH BUILT THROUGHOUT.
Full particulars from:
LAGONDA LIMITED
195, Hammersmith Road, LONDON, W.6.
Telephone: Hammersmith 575.
Telegrams: "Lagondy, Hammer, London."
Head Office and Works   -   -   STAINES.

£410

CARR'S
TABLE WATER
BISCUITS
are not the ordinary water biscuits. Try them and you will appreciate the difference.
MADE ONLY BY
CARR & CO. LTD
CARLISLE

LEFT AND OPPOSITE: Cars of all sizes to suit every budget. All of these adverts appeared on the same page of *The Times*, 1924.

Rocking Armchair No. 11.

Child's Armchair No. 2 Child's Chair No. 1.
with playboard.

Child's high tablechair No. 1.

Rocking Armchair No. 4.

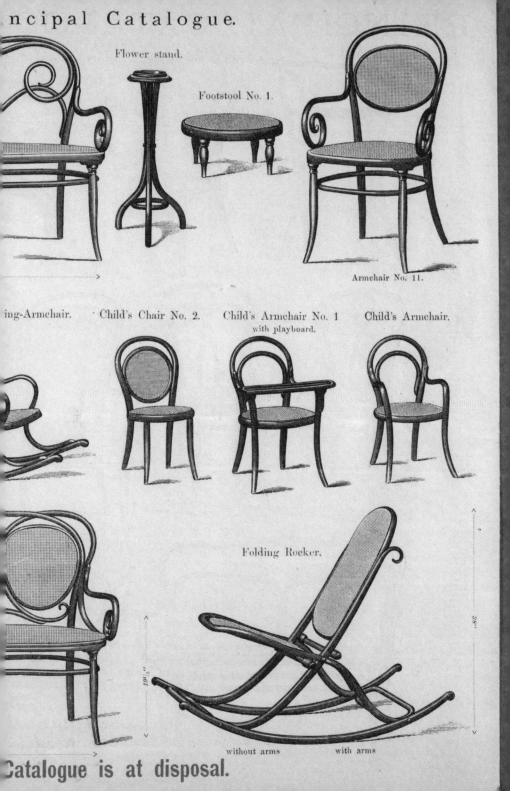

Flower stand.

Footstool No. 1.

Armchair No. 11.

ing-Armchair. · Child's Chair No. 2. Child's Armchair No. 1
with playboard. Child's Armchair.

Folding Rocker.

without arms   with arms

PREVIOUS PAGES: 'Our furnitures with patent leg joint are put up easely [sic] by anybody'. Kohn's undestroyable Vienna bent wood furniture, c. 1885.

WHEN ON THE LOOK OUT
For Reliable Remedies for Rheumatism, Chills, Influenza, Liver and Kidney Complaints;

Bear in mind that

HOLLOWAY'S
PILLS AND OINTMENT
always rout the Enemy

Can you do this — to-day?

TOP RIGHT: Holloway's Pills are a testament to the power of advertising. By the time of his death Thomas Holloway was spending £50,000 a year on advertising his patent medicines, and died a very rich man indeed. Holloway's Pills were later bought up by the rival firm Beecham's. This advert appeared in The Universal Magazine, 1900.

RIGHT: The promise of health. Ryvita, Britannia & Eve, 1929.

OPPOSITE: 'It will prove a source of unlimited interest in every house and home'. Thacker's Patent Home Gymnasium, c. 1885.

WOULDN'T you be glad to have back the suppleness you once had . . . the easy, springy step . . . the litheness you never valued until it was too late?

We cannot stop Time. But we can carry many of the advantages of youth (slimness, for instance) into middle age—even into old age.

That is, indeed, just what "Ryvita Crispbread" helps us to do.

By making you fit and keeping you slim, "Ryvita" makes you younger and keeps you younger.

By giving vigour to your digestion, it keeps you vigorous. By nourishing muscle, bone and sinew, it makes you hardy, able to resist illness and disease. By helping in the absorption and elimination of fat and starchy foods, it enables you to retain elasticity and poise; whether your age is 25, 45 or 65.

Try "Ryvita"—the wonderful daily bread of Sweden.

Eat some every day. It's delicious with butter, cheese, jam, marmalade, celery—or with milk to make rye-porridge. But it is more than a delightful food, it is a complete food, rich in phosphates and vitamins. Eat "Ryvita" and your daily bread and you need never really part from Youth.

"Ryvita Crispbread" is sold by all good grocers and stores at 1/6 per 40-50 slice (1-lb.) cartons; also in ½-lb. cartons, 10d.

"RYVITA CRISPBREAD"
—makes you fit and keeps you slim

FREE SAMPLE

CUT AND POST NOW
RYVITA CO. (482) RYVITA HOUSE, 96, SOUTHWARK STREET S.E.1
Please send Sample and Ryvita Book Free to—
NAME .... Write very plainly
CUT AND POST TO-
DAY ½d. STAMP ADDRESS ....

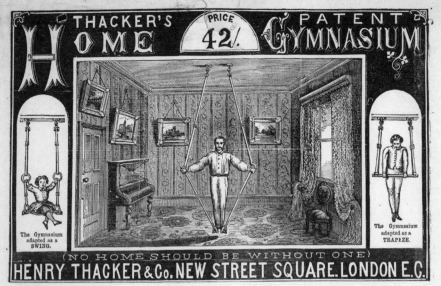

THACKER'S **HOME** PATENT **GYMNASIUM**

PRICE 42/

The Gymnasium adapted as a SWING.

The Gymnasium adapted as a TRAPEZE.

(NO HOME SHOULD BE WITHOUT ONE)

HENRY THACKER & Co. NEW STREET SQUARE. LONDON E.C.

NEW STREET SQUARE,
LONDON, E.C.

Dear Sir,

We desire to call your attention to our PATENT HOME GYMNASIUM, which has had a very large sale during the past 10 years. It can be put up in any room, and can be removed in one minute; a room 6 or 8 feet square will give ample space for every exercise. It is constructed with special regard to strength and is suitable alike for Children, Grown Persons, and Ladies. It is supported by two Strong Hooks in the ceiling, which are screwed into the joist 5 inches, leaving only the small hooks visible. Any carpenter can fit them in a short time. It can be converted at pleasure into a Horizontal Bar, Trapeze Bar, Hand Rings, Stirrup Exercises, or a Swing. An Illustrated Handbook containing 220 Exercises, each one Illustrated, and all Attachments, Complete, with Directions, accompany each Gymnasium, in box.

This Gymnasium is alike suitable for the Parlour, Nursery, Bedroom, Study, or School-Room. All the bars, ladders, swings, etc., of the ordinary Gymnasium, will not give the variety which is found in this single and simple apparatus. It is justly esteemed the most remarkable invention in the whole field of physical culture. It is adapted to persons of all ages and both sexes, and to the wants of all those who cannot avail themselves of the advantages of a Gymnastic Institution. It will prove a source of unlimited interest in every house and home.

The question of physical education—long a matter of abstract and experimental investigation —has now assumed a position in the public esteem, commensurate with its importance; and all who have investigated the matter are convinced that it should be promoted in our schools and homes. All complete Gymnasiums that have been previously constructed, have been too cumbrous or too expensive; and those of a cheap and simple character have been lacking in the necessary scope and variety, not being adatped to swinging or somersault exercises. Many attempts have been made to construct one which would overcome these difficulties; and this we now claim to have accomplished in our PATENT HOME GYMNASIUM. It is constructed with special regard to the true principle of physical culture, and we only ask for it a thorough, scientific examination. The anatomist, in examining the exercises, will not fail to discover that each and every set of muscles has received studied attention. Every joint and muscle is exercised under healthful conditions, and while the first exercises are simple enough for children, the last are such as can only be accomplished by those who are in downright earnest. It must, therefore, become the means of unlimited generalization of gymnastic exercise.

To Clergymen, Literary Men, and all persons of sedentary occupations, it is particularly adapted. The exercises are especially invigorating to the digestive and respiratory organs.

For Colleges, Schools, Children, and Families it is of the greatest service. To children it is a means of healthful recreation and enjoyment.

To Invalids and Persons of Delicate Health it is a great boon. The feeble are constantly advised to take exercise: but the difficulty is to find an easy means of doing so. This Gymnasium supplies this desideratum. It is also of great value in creating the necessary reaction after a bath.

We will forward a Gymnasium, Carriage Paid, on receipt of Cheque, or Post Office Order, for £2 2s. 0d. Cheques crossed "City Bank," and Post Office Orders made payable at Ludgate Circus.

Trusting we may receive the favour of your order,

We remain, dear Sir,

Respectfully Yours,

Henry Thacker & Co

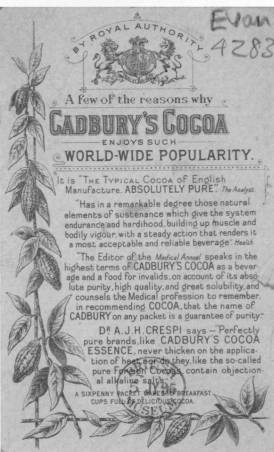

Evan
4283

BY ROYAL AUTHORITY

A few of the reasons why

CADBURY'S COCOA

ENJOYS SUCH

WORLD-WIDE POPULARITY.

It is "The Typical Cocoa of English Manufacture, ABSOLUTELY PURE". *The Analyst.*

"Has in a remarkable degree those natural elements of sustenance which give the system endurance and hardihood, building up muscle and bodily vigour, with a steady action that renders it a most acceptable and reliable beverage". *Health.*

"The Editor of the *Medical Annual* speaks in the highest terms of CADBURY'S COCOA as a beverage and a food for invalids, on account of its absolute purity, high quality, and great solubility, and counsels the Medical profession to remember, in recommending COCOA, that the name of CADBURY on any packet is a guarantee of purity".

Dʀ A.J.H.CRESPI says – "Perfectly pure brands, like CADBURY'S COCOA ESSENCE, never thicken on the application of heat, nor do they, like the so-called pure Foreign Cocoas, contain objectional alkaline salts".

A SIXPENNY PACKET MAKES 40 BREAKFAST CUPS FULL OF DELICIOUS COCOA.

OPPOSITE AND RIGHT: The front and back of a trade card for Cadbury's Cocoa, *c.* 1885.

CADBURY'S COCOA

THE TYPICAL COCOA OF ENGLISH
MANUFACTURE ABSOLUTELY PURE—
(THE ANALYST)

NO CHEMICALS USED
(AS IN THE SO CALLED
PURE FOREIGN COCOAS.)

H. BLACKLOCK & C° PRINTERS. MANCHESTER.

Naval Manoeuvres.

ABOVE AND OPPOSITE: The romance
of chocolate. Fry's milk chocolate,
The Sphere, November 1909.
Rowntree's York Assortment,
Britannia & Eve, 1929.

Jack bought a box of
Rowntree's YORK Chocolates

Mary came in !!!

Rowntree's famous York Chocolates; in 1-lb. boxes, 4/-; and in cartons, ½-lb. 2/-, ¾-lb. 1/-.

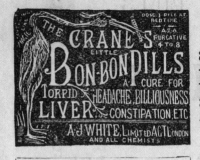

O N S.— Cranes
Bon Pills operate
as a Purgative
f 3 to 4.   In ex-
es 6 and even 8
ken.

n-Bon Pill every
cure obstinate
on.

n-Bon Pill at bed-
ire a Headache.

night will remove
e in the Mouth.

vill cure Pain in

dinner pill will
ss after Eating.

will cure Dizzi-

vill cure Drowsi-

will remove the
n.

f Cranes Little
ills will break up

ll cure Bilious-

'ills are purely
and harmless,
orough, causing
r distress.

a Bottle.

TE, LIMITED,
GDON ROAD
DON.

LEFT: Military practicality is the order of the day. Blanco, *John Bull*, 1917.

BELOW LEFT: Even beauty products adjusted their slogans for the war years. *Punch*, 1918.

BELOW RIGHT: 'that unmistakable soldier-cut'. Thresher & Glenny Military Tailors, *The Sphere*, 1917.

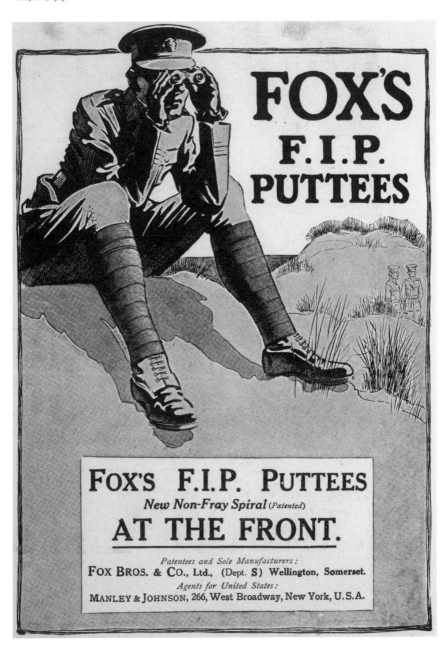

Take a Kodak with you.

First Lady :— *Why Baby's Complexion is the Envy of the Rose, and how like its mother!*

Second Lady :— *Well, you know the secret — Pears!*

ABOVE: 'You know the secret – Pears!', *The Queen*, 1914.

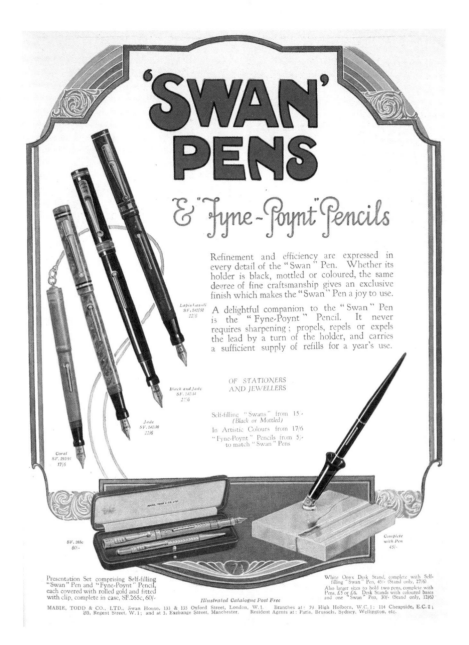

'SWAN' PENS

& "Fyne-Poynt" Pencils

Refinement and efficiency are expressed in every detail of the "Swan" Pen. Whether its holder is black, mottled or coloured, the same degree of fine craftsmanship gives an exclusive finish which makes the "Swan" Pen a joy to use.

A delightful companion to the "Swan" Pen is the "Fyne-Poynt" Pencil. It never requires sharpening; propels, repels or expels the lead by a turn of the holder, and carries a sufficient supply of refills for a year's use.

Lapis Lazuli SF. 242/32 22/6

Black and Jade SF. 242/34 22/6

Jade SF. 242/30 22/6

Coral SF. 292/91 17/6

OF STATIONERS
AND JEWELLERS

Self-filling "Swans" from 15 -
(Black or Mottled)
In Artistic Colours from 17/6
"Fyne-Poynt" Pencils from 5/-
to match "Swan" Pens

SF. 265c 60/-

Complete with Pen 45/-

Presentation Set comprising Self-filling "Swan" Pen and "Fyne-Poynt" Pencil, each covered with rolled gold and fitted with clip, complete in case, SF.265c, 60/-

Illustrated Catalogue Post Free

White Onyx Desk Stand, complete with Self-filling "Swan" Pen, 45/- (Stand only, 27/6) Also larger sizes to hold two pens, complete with Pens, £5 or £6. Desk Stands with coloured bases and one "Swan" Pen, 30/- (Stand only, 12/6)

MABIE, TODD & CO., LTD., Swan House, 133 & 135 Oxford Street, London, W.1. Branches at: 79 High Holborn, W.C.1; 114 Cheapside, E.C.2; 95, Regent Street, W.1; and at 3, Exchange Street, Manchester. Resident Agents at: Paris, Brussels, Sydney, Wellington, etc.

OPPOSITE: Trade card for Cadbury's Cocoa, c. 1885.

ABOVE: 'Swan' Pens and 'Fyne-Poynt' Pencils, *The Tatler*, 1929.

79

BEECHAM'S PILLS

Give
Health
&
Vigour

Beecham's Pills helped create a global
pharmaceutical company. They were first
marketed *c.* 1842 and remained in production
until 1998.

ABOVE: 'Health & Vigour', *Illustrated Sporting
and Dramatic News*, 1914.

OPPOSITE: 'Save the Constitution', *Illustrated
Sporting and Dramatic News*, 1896.

Guard Yourself

AND

Save the Constitution

BY TAKING

BEECHAM'S PILLS,

The National Medicine

ONE OUNCE IS GUARANTEED TO CONTAIN MORE REAL & DIRECT NOURISHMENT THAN 50 OUNCES OF LIEBIGS OR ANY SIMILAR EXTRACT OF BEEF

JOHNSTON'S

THE MOST PERFECT FORM OF
CONCENTRATED NOURISHMENT
AT PRESENT KNOWN.
10 TRINITY SQ. TOWER HILL. LONDON
FLUID BEEF

ONE OUNCE IS GUARANTEED TO CONTAIN
THE MOST PERFECT FORM OF
CONCENTRATED NOURISHMENT
AT PRESENT KNOWN.
10 TRINITY SQ. TOWER HILL. LONDON
JOHNSTON'S FLUID BEEF

WATERPROOF CYCLING CAPES, COATS, &c.

LATEST APPROVED SHAPES FOR GENTLEMEN AND LADIES.

The Beeston Cape, 8/6 to 13/6.   The Ideal Cape, with Apron attached, 13/6 to 18/6.

The Princess Coat, loose sleeves, 21/- to 30/-   Gentlemen's Waterproofs, new shapes, from 21/- to 90/-

ꓑETER ROBINSON, LTD. 204 to 212 OXFORD-ST.

ABOVE: Weather was no deterrent to the new fashion for cycling. *The Illustrated Sporting and Dramatic News*, 1896.

OPPOSITE: Tea, the drink of the Empire. Men representing China, India, Ceylon and Assam offer crates of tea to Britannia. *Illustrated London News*, 1894.

OPPOSITE: Wright's Coal Tar Soap,
The Queen, Xmas 1914.

ABOVE: Brooke's Monkey Brand
Soap, *Pears Pictorial Christmas*,
1899.

ELLIMAN'S

READ the Elliman E.F.A. Booklet 72 pp enclosed in the wrappers of bottles of Ellimans Royal Embrocation for use on animals, 1/- 2/- & 3/6

READ the Elliman R.E.P. Booklet 96 pp. illustrated, which accompanies bottles of Elliman's Universal Embrocation for Human use, 1/1½ & 2/9

ELLIMAN

ELLIMAN'S

READ Page 1 of the Elliman R. E. P. Booklet, 96 pp. illustrated, which accompanies bottles of Elliman's Universal Embrocation for Human use, 1/1½ & 2/9
Page 1 of the Elliman E. F. A. Booklet, 72 pp., enclosed in the wrappers of bottles of Elliman's Royal Embrocation for use on Animals, 1/-, 2/- & 3/6

ELLIMAN, SONS & CO., EMBROCATION MANUFACTURERS, SLOUGH, ENGLAND.

OPPOSITE AND ABOVE: Elliman, Sons & Co. made two products: Royal Embrocation for use on animals and Universal Embrocation for use on humans. Made from eggs, turpentine and vinegar, the recipe was the same for both. Elliman's universal muscle rub is still produced today (to a slightly different recipe).

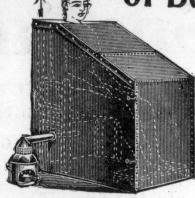
ABOVE: Foot & Son's folding bath cabinet, *Illustrated London News*, 1900.

OPPOSITE: From 'Bubbles' to 'Impudence', Pears knew the appeal of a cute child in advertising. *Pears' Pictorial Christmas*, 1899.

Pears' Soap

"IMPUDENCE"

M°Corquedale & C° Limited.London.

PATENTEES & SOLE MANUFACTURERS } J. S

LEFT: More Victorian ingenuity. Stone's Patent 'Automatic' fold-up lavatory, 1882. One wonders how it was 'automatic'.

& C?

)RD, LONDON. S.E.

PICOTEE SHOES FOR WOMEN

ABOVE AND OPPOSITE: Women's shoes
advertisements, *Footwear Organiser*, 1919.

ABOVE: A variation on the three
birds logo still in use today. Bird's
Custard, *Britannia & Eve*, 1929.

OPPOSITE: Hammering home the
point. A 'gipsy queen' in Gipsy
Queen shoes, aboard the 'Gipsy
Queen'. *Footwear Organiser*, 1919.

GIPSY QUEEN SHOES

RETAIL AGENTS APPOINTED

Manufacturers :

WILKES BROS. & CO. ⸱ LEICESTER

ABOVE: Golden Dawn sandals for that Greek Goddess look. *Footwear Organiser*, 1919.

LEFT: 'A dainty necessity to be carried in every hand-bag', Powderette DuBarry, *The Times of India*, Christmas issue 1919.

LEFT: 'Renowned for durability, reliability and comparative cheapness', Muir Mills offered everything a member of the Raj could want in textiles. *The Times of India*, Christmas issue, 1919.

ABOVE: Luxurious travel to far-flung
destinations became more common
in the inter-war years. This advert
for Egypt comes from *Britannia &
Eve*, 1929.

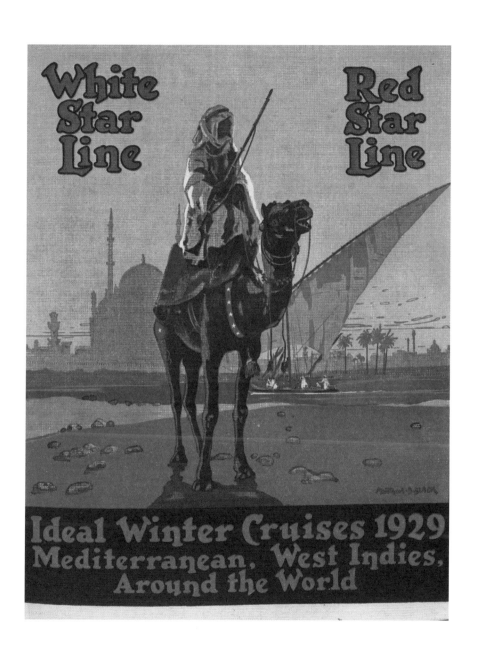

White
Star
Line

Red
Star
Line

Ideal Winter Cruises 1929
Mediterranean, West Indies,
Around the World

ABOVE: The lure of the exotic.
Booklet cover for Ideal Winter
Cruises, designed by Montague
B. Black, 1929.

ABOVE: She might be clean but she doesn't look very happy. Fairy Soap, *Puck*, 1915.

OPPOSITE: Plimsolls and sand shoes for summer holidays. *Footwear Organiser*, 1919.

PLIMSOLLS & SAND SHOES

LARGE STOCKS ALWAYS

CUNARD

S.S. "AQUITANIA"

S. S. LUSITANIA   S. S. MAURETANIA
THE WORLD'S FASTEST STEAMERS

THE PUCK PRESS

In the wake
of the
Merchant
Adventurers

Cunard
Winter Cruises

OPPOSITE: Cunard's transatlantic
crossings, *Puck*, 22 May 1915.
The S.S. Lusitania had just been
torpedoed (7 May 1915), although
the advert had probably already
gone to print.

ABOVE: Cunard Winter Cruises,
poster designed by Thomas Carr,
1929.

ABOVE: Clarke's 'Cricklite' Lamps held candles in glass domes, and were advertised for use as table decorations for special occasions. *Pears Pictorial Christmas*, 1899.

for burning Clarke's
Trade Mark "Cricklite".

The Pierce Arrow

FOR 1910, four types of cars, limousine, touring, miniature tonneau and runabout. Three horse-powers, 36, 48 and 66—all six cylinder.

THE PIERCE-ARROW MOTOR CAR CO., BUFFALO, N. Y.
Members Association Licensed Automobile Manufacturers

ABOVE: Pierce-Arrow cars were unashamedly upmarket and luxurious. Unlike most car adverts, the car is in the background and not fully visible. A wealthy, fashionable lady strides forth, wallet open to shop, the car having just conveyed her there. *Colliers*, 1909.

HILLMAN-
AGAIN AHEAD
WONDERFUL NEW MODELS SET FASHION FOR 1930

FEATURES

Chromium Plating

"Silentbloc" oil-less shackles

Dipping Headlights

Thermostatic Radiator *

Four-speed Gear Box,

Finger light steering,

Reserve Petrol Supply,

Ample Room.

New colour schemes.

(" Straight Eight " only *)

HILLMAN "STRAIGHT EIGHT"

FROM £430

HILLMAN "FOURTEEN"

FROM £310

The 1930 Hillman models set a new fashion in line and luxury, performance and price. To the low-slung, comfortable Hillmans, that everyone has been admiring this season, have now been added many extra refinements. Increased flexibility, speed and acceleration, better springing and upholstery, " Silentbloc" rubber shackles, chromium plating throughout and a host of other improvements establish the new Hillmans more firmly than ever as the ideal combination of comfort, appearance, performance and price. Why not try the new Hillmans at once and be among the first to enjoy this newer, higher standard of motoring? Full colour catalogue of new models (publication H/30) post free on request.

MODELS FROM

£310

HC 1930

THE HILLMAN MOTOR
CAR Co., Ltd., Coventry.

World Exporters:
ROOTES LTD.,
Devonshire House, Piccadilly,
London, W. 1.

HILLMAN

THE CAR THAT COSTS LESS THAN IT SHOULD

ABOVE: Here the emphasis is on
affordability, with the car the
only image on the page. Hillman,
Britannia & Eve, 1929.

FIGHTING FOR
PATENT FOOD LONDON
TRADE MARK
DR. RIDGE'S
PATENT COOKED FOOD
GIVES

RIDGE'S FOOD

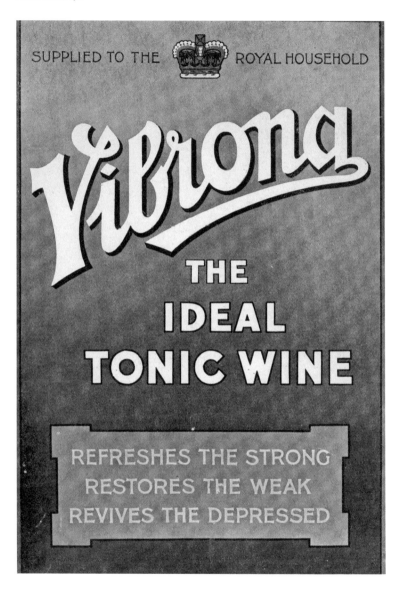

SUPPLIED TO THE ROYAL HOUSEHOLD

Vibrona

THE IDEAL TONIC WINE

REFRESHES THE STRONG
RESTORES THE WEAK
REVIVES THE DEPRESSED

ABOVE: At 19.3% alcohol, the reviving, restorative effects of this tonic wine were probably relatively short-lived. *Times of India*, 1919.

OPPOSITE: It might 'save time', but 'making washing a pleasure' may be a claim too far. *Illustrated London News*, 1902.

SUNLIGHT SOAP

"Not yet One And Washing Done"

NLIGHT SOAP Saves time.

LIGHT SOAP Lengthens life.

LIGHT SOAP Adds to the joys of home.

SUNLIGHT SOAP

Reduces the Hours of Labour.

Increases the Hours of Ease.

LARGEST SALE IN THE WORLD.

SUNLIGHT SOAP Makes washing a pleasure.

SUNLIGHT SOAP Gives rest and comfort.

SUNLIGHT SOAP Preserves the clothes.

LEVER BROTHERS, LIMITED, PORT SUNLIGHT, CHESHIRE.

ABOVE: From sponsoring the athletes in the 1908 Olympics to nurturing school-children, Oxo advertising was firmly focused on its health-giving benefits. *Britannia & Eve*, 1929.

OPPOSITE: Who needs safety ropes? A cup of Fry's cocoa will see you to the top of the mountain. *The Sphere*, 1910.

John!
don't forget my '25' box
of Craven "A

The only cigarettes that do not affect my throat

OPPOSITE: Craven 'A' cigarettes had cork tips at a time when most brands did not contain filters. Adverts claimed that they prevented sore throats. *Britannia & Eve*, 1929.

ABOVE AND RIGHT: Whether for fashionable ladies going shooting on the glorious twelfth (*The Queen*, 1909*)*, or naval officers during WWI (*The Bystander*, 1914), a Burberrys coat was the garment to be seen in. Thomas Burberry introduced the hard-wearing, water-resistant fabric gabardine, in 1880. The Tielocken coat was patented in 1912 and was the predecessor to the iconic trench coat.

Try this Delightful Summer Drink

TRY this really delightful drink for summer days— cold "Ovaltine." As delicious in this way as when made as a hot beverage. It not merely quenches the thirst but refreshes and invigorates as well. It supplies, too, the nourishment you particularly need in the summer — for ordinary hot weather foods contain little nourishment, while the need for nourishment remains much the same all the year round.

Cold "Ovaltine" is easy to prepare. Add to cold milk or milk and water. Whisk with an egg-whisk or shake in a cocktail shaker. Then you have a creamy, foaming drink—as delicious as it is refreshing. Brimful, too, of energy-giving nourishment to enable you to avoid fatigue and to keep vigorous and healthy.

'OVALTINE'
Nourishing COLD & Refreshing

P363

Obtainable throughout the British Empire.   Prices in Great Britain and Northern Ireland 1/3, 2/- and 3/9 per tin.

ABOVE: Not just a warm drink for bedtime. *Britannia & Eve*, 1929.

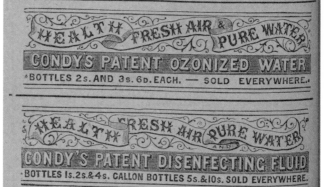
ABOVE: Advertisments from the back pages of Beeton's *The Mother's Home-Book*, 1871.

OPPOSITE: All the latest oil-fuelled gadgets for the home. Handbill, 1883.

CHARLES GOSLING'S
Excelsior, Stove, and Lamp Works,
107, GREAT SUFFOLK STREET, BOROUGH, LONDON.

Oct -13

HEATING, COOKING, AND IRONING BY PETROLEUM OIL.
(Protected by Her Majesty's Royal Letters Patent.)

This is the little Napoleon Stove for boiling a quart of water or for cooking eggs, by means of methylated spirits

No. 0 Stove. This Stove is a jem, no house should be without it, by it you can cook any small article of food, boil water, keep infants food warm, toast muffins or bread and if you wish you can by removing the top, convert it into a parafin lamp, which gives a most brilliant light, as shewn in engraving to the right

This is the No. 0 Stove converted into a lamp simply by removing the top and placing the glass in its place, this is quite a boon for the poor and of equal benefit to the rich. A person may cook what they want in the day, and convert it into a lamp for the evening, the cost of burning being about two-pence per week

This represents the Excelsior Night Light, which will burn for Eight-hours & cost but one half-penny per week

No. 1 Stove suitable for a small family by which you can boil half a gallon of water, bake a small joint, or boil vegetables.

No. 3, this represents the Stove with top thrown back ready for lighting.

Grid and Cover. This is suitable for either No. 2, 3, or 4, Stove and needs but one trial to do away with the old method of frying meats or fish. Steaks or Chops grilled on this, retain all their natural juices and flavour, and are much more delicious than when grilled over the ordinary coal fire.

No. 2, Stove with Saucepan.

No. 2, Stove with Grid, as shown in illustration over heading Grid and Cover. This is a most economical way of cooking

No. 2 Stove with Saucepan & Steamer, this is a very useful Stove and cooks at a very small cost.

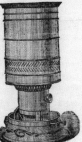

The No. 3 is here represented with the New Heating Cylinder, which is well adapted for heating small conservatories, bath-rooms, bed-chambers, green-houses, &c. This is a most excellent article, giving a nice moist heat, without ashes or dirt to carry out, it can be regulated so as to give a small or greater amount of heat as may be required.

No. 3 Stove with Kettle in which a gallon of water can be boiled in sixteen minuets.

No. 3 Stove with Iron Heater. This is considered one of the most important improvements of the period, you can place the Stove by your side or on the table, and for one half-penny per hour, iron your clothes with dispatch; and not suffer the distressing effects of heat, as you do over an ordinary stove or range. No woman, having once tried this, would be without it for double its price.—Try it !

No. 3 Stove with wash boiler attached, which is a new and novel way of washing

No. 3 Stove with Steam Cooking Apparatus, by which means three articles can be cooked by steam and two boiled, this is a most useful Stove.

No. 4 Stove which is two No. 3's on one tray by which you can bake two articles at the same time and also cook your vegetables or boil a kettle. This Stove will cook for any family at the cost of one half-penny per hour.

NOTICE.—It must be thoroughly understood that these STOVES are sold seperate, and that the various ware can be used on the same Stove—thus, you can remove

HAMLEY'S LATEST

LATEST PUZZLE.

Write for New

The **Way to Constantinople**, the most ingenious and tantalizing puzzle on the market. **8/3** dozen or **96/-** gross.

Hamley's Patriotic MASCOT Fi men, Fine Window

EXPLODING

HA

86/7.

RITISH NOVELTIES

lesale List.

Perfect models of our leading
n. Price **9/4½** each.

Trench Football, a most exciting
puzzle. Fun, Skill and Dexterity.
Price **8/-** dozen, in lots 12 dozen, **7/9**.

CH. Upon the Flag being struck, there is a loud explosion and
ldiers are thrown in all directions. Price, **30/-** dozen.

EY BROS., LTD.,

gh Holborn, London, W.C.

— "And some have greatness thrust upon them."

BIRD'S CUSTARD
makes children sturdy!

PREVIOUS PAGES: Hamley's, the world's oldest toy shop, first opened in 1760. Here the horrors of the trenches are reduced to patriotic games. *Games and Toys*, 1915.

ABOVE: Custard is the magic ingredient for sturdy little boys. *The Strand*, 1927.

OPPOSITE: Marmite's early publicity campaigns emphasised the spread's healthy nature. Poster designed by J. Woolley, 1929.

MARMITE

For Health and Good Cooking

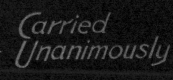

Carried Unanimously

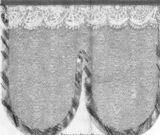

The absolute ...

ALL=BRITISH FIRM

Compocastles Ltd.,

108, Upper Street, London, N.

'Phone :
3338 North.

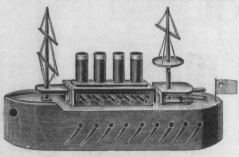

DREADNOUGHT

28 inches long   -   -   **90/-** per dozen.

COMPOCASTLES' NEW GUN

(*Patent Pending.*)

Enormous Range.   Terrific Report.
Fires Rubber Shells.   Quite Harmless.

A magnificent model.   Stocks in preparation

Particulars on request.

TOY FORTS, from 6d. to 50 Guineas.
CASTLES, DOLLS' HOUSES, MODEL COTTAGES.

NEW LINES.

Toy Rifles, Howitzers, Cannon, Engines, Pigeon Shooting Game, Mysteriscopes, Toy Bedsteads, Tunnels, Shelter Trenches, Camp Stools.

NEW LIST ON REQUEST.

OPPOSITE: Advertising leaflet for the Vertical
Feed Sewing Machine, 1883.

ABOVE: More military toys for the patriotic
child of WWI. *Games and Toys*, 1915.

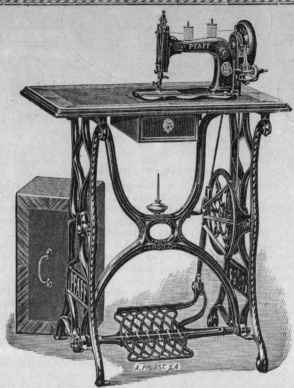

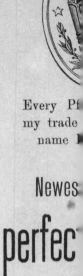
The Pfaff „B" Perfect Sewing Machine.
High Arm Family-Machine.

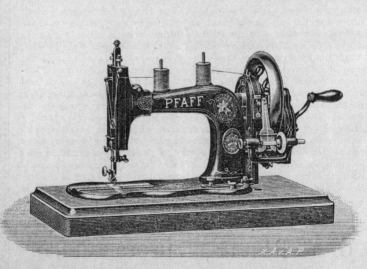

The Pfaff „B" Perfect Sewing Machine.
High Arm Family Handmachine on wood base.

Mark.

ine bears
d also the
the arm.

ement:

iseless

ll

cost.

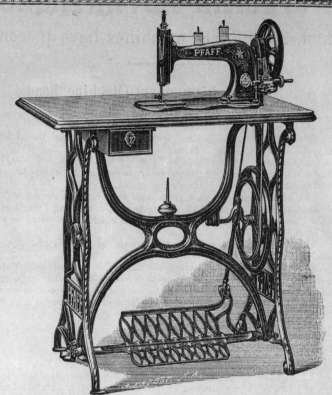

The Pfaff „C" Tailoring Machine.
High Arm Medium Machine.

arts sub-
forged of
t cast.

ges see

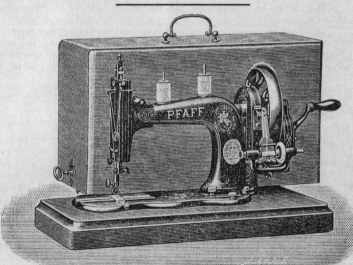

The Pfaff „B" Perfect Sewing Machine.
High Arm Family Handmachine on wood base with handsome Walnut cover.

"The kind that won't dry on the face !"

FOR a good many years—depending on how old you are—you've been hearing that Williams' lather "won't dry on the face." Have you ever stopped to think just what that signifies? Of course it doesn't mean that after getting all lathered up you can stop to play with the baby for half an hour, or run to a fire. But it does mean that you can put on the rich, softening, creamy lather, strop your razor well, go all the way round at a leisurely pace, and finish off a velvety shave without having to lather the face a second time. That is the reason why a Williams' shave is both quicker and more comfortable. Get Williams' convenient Holder-Top Shaving Stick and try it to-morrow.

Holder Top Shaving Stick

Williams Luxury Shaving Cream

Stick

WILLIAMS' TALC POWDER
COOLING — SOOTHING
DELIGHTFUL TO USE
AFTER SHAVING.
OFFERED IN SEVERAL
EXQUISITE PERFUMES

Cream

Williams Quick & Easy Shaving Powder

Williams Shaving Liquid

Powder

Liquid

Williams' Holder Top Shaving Stick

THE J.B.WILLIAMS COMPANY, GLASTONBURY, CONN. U.S. AMERICA.

SOLE REPRESENTATIVES FOR INDIA
Muller & Phipps (India) Ltd., Bombay, Calcutta, Madras, Karachi, Lahore, Delhi, Amritsar & Rangoon.
Muller & Phipps (Asia) Ltd., Colombo, Ceylon.
Muller Phipps & Sellers, Ltd., Singapore, S.S.

PREVIOUS PAGES: Among the 'Special Advantages' listed on the other side of this sheet is the claim that 'it is made impossible that a machine leaving the works can have the least imperfection'! Advertising leaflet for Pfaff sewing machines, c. 1885.

ABOVE: A 'quicker and more comfortable' shave. *The Times of India Illustrated Weekly,* 1919.

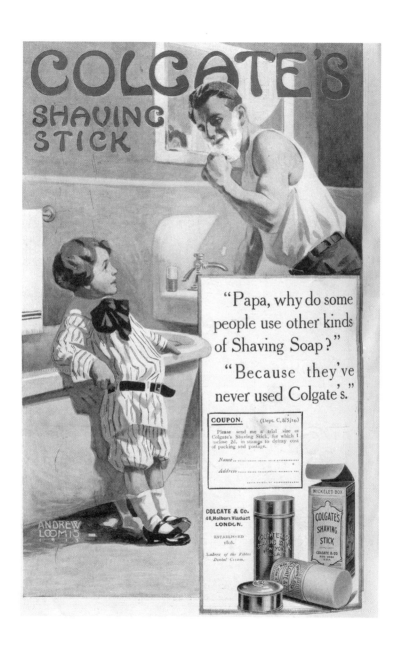

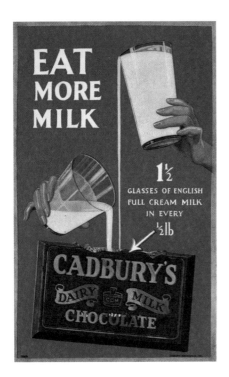

LEFT: The iconic 'glass and a half' measure of milk was first used to advertise Cadbury's Dairy Milk in 1928. Eighty plus years later and Cadbury's TV commercials are produced by an in-house team known as 'Glass & a Half Full Productions'.

BELOW LEFT: The famous slogan was coined by the agency SH Benson and first appeared in 1929. Apparently punters in London pubs were asked 'Why are you drinking Guinness?' and the reply was usually 'Guinness is good for you'. *Britannia & Eve*, 1929.

OPPOSITE: Perfection, no matter how far away you are. *Times of India Illustrated Weekly*, 1919.

D & J. Mc CALLUM'S

Perfection

SCOTCH WHISKY.

SHELL

FOR THE UTMOST
HORSE POWER

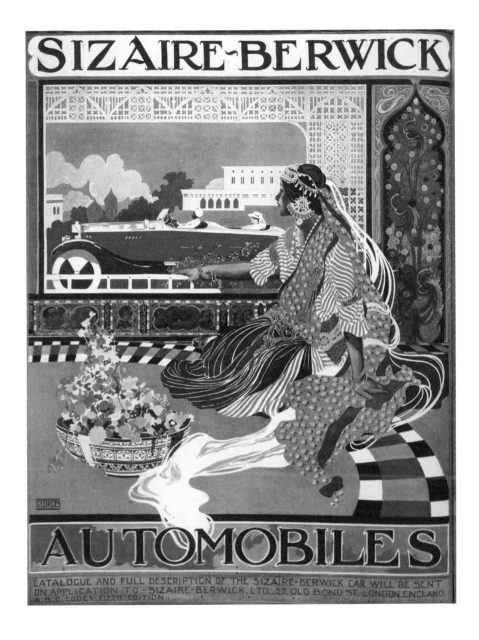

SIZAIRE-BERWICK

AUTOMOBILES

CATALOGUE AND FULL DESCRIPTION OF THE SIZAIRE-BERWICK CAR WILL BE SENT ON APPLICATION TO - SIZAIRE-BERWICK. LTD., 27. OLD BOND ST. LONDON. ENGLAND. A.B.C. CODES FIFTH EDITION.

OPPOSITE: 'Iron Horse' poster designed for Shell by Jean d'Ylen, 1926.

ABOVE: The car of choice for Maharajahs. *Times of India Illustrated Weekly*, 1919.

IMPORTANT NOTICE TO LADIES.

Evan.
8129

THE MARCH NUMBER OF THE

LONDON JOURNAL FASHIONS

(PRICE ONE PENNY)

Will contain a Full-size Cut-out Paper Pattern of a

FASHIONABLE DRESS BODICE,

Illustration of which is given below.

THE EUGÉNIE BODICE.

This number will also contain a great variety of Illustrations of the Latest Paris Fashions, by the most eminent Parisian artists. Full descriptions of each will be given, including quantities of materials to be used in making up, besides a variety of useful information.

☞ This number will be published on February 16th, so please give an order to your Newsvendor at once to supply you with a copy.

C. W. BRADLEY & CO., 12 & 13, FETTER LANE, LONDON.

FARM DAIRY.

W. H. DANIELL

Cowkeeper,

Brooke Street, Holborn,

And 14, Francis Street,

TOTTENHAM COURT ROAD.

ABOVE: Paper bag printed with an advertisement for a dairy farm in what is now Central London, 1881.

Insure yo

GUARDIAN HORSE VEHICLE &

LI

31, LOMBARD ST

10, St. Andrew

Registered C

P

The Most Noble The MARQUIS OF HEADFORT.
The Right Honourable The EARL OF CHARLEMONT.
The Right Honourable The EARL OF CLONMEL.
The Right Honourable The EARL OF HUNTINGDON, M.F.H.
The Right Honourable The EARL OF WICKLOW.
The Right Honourable VISCOUNT MASSEREENE.
The Right Honourable LORD CLONCURRY.
LORD RANDOLPH CHURCHILL, M.P.
LORD FERMOY.
LORD ORANMORE and BROWNE.
LORD CLANMORRIS.
SIR ROBERT PIGOT, Bart.
MAJOR SIR ERASMUS BURROWES, Bart.
SIR DAVID VANDELEUR ROCHE, Bart., M.F.H.

DIRECTORS IN LONDON.

RICHARD ATTENBOROUGH, Esq., *Chairman.*
R. FARQUHARSON, Esq., M.D., M.P.
H. W. MAYNARD, Esq., London.
CAPTAIN MIREHOUSE, J.P., Bristol.
SIR ROSE L. PRICE, Bart.
COMMANDER G. E. PRICE, R.N., M.P.
FITZHERBERT WRIGHT, Esq., J.P., Alfretou.

BANKERS.

NATIONAL PROVINCIAL BANK OF ENGLAND.

ur Horses

...IE ...ENERAL INSURANCE COMPANY,

...ED,

...ET, LONDON, E.C.,

...are, Edinburgh.

...al, £100,000.

...NS.

SIR HUGH CHOLMELEY, Bart., M.P.
GENERAL W. H. SEYMOUR, C.B., Late 2nd Dragoon Guards.
LIEUT.-GENERAL ROBERT WARDLAW.
COLONEL FORSTER, Master of the Horse to H. E. The Lord
    Lieutenant of Ireland.
COLONEL FRANK CHAPLIN, M.F.H.
MAJOR The HONOURABLE FREDERICK TRENCH.
CAPTAIN J. McCALMONT, A.D.C., Late 8th Hussars.
LEONARD MORROGH, Esq., Master of the Ward Hunt.
WILLIAM KILLIGREW WAIT, Esq.
WILLIAM NEWCOME WALLER, Esq., M.F.H.
BURTON R. P. PERSSE, Esq., M.F.H.
WILLIAM DE SALLIS FILGATE, Esq., M.F.H.

DIRECTORS IN SCOTLAND.

R. FARQUHARSON, Esq., M.D., M.P. (of Finzean), *Chairman.*
ANDREW GILLON, Esq., J.P., D.L. (of Wallhouse), *Deputy-Chairman.*
A. H. FERRYMAN, Esq., J.P. (of Lochend).
LIEUT.-COL. J. S. RYLEY (Director Edinburgh Tramway Co.)
LIEUT.-COL. DUNBAR.
JOHN KETCHER, Esq. (of Salton.)

GENERAL MANAGER.
ERNEST H. WILSON, Esq.

ASK FOR "The Morning" THE HALFPENNY MORNING NEWSPAPER.

OPPOSITE AND ABOVE: When holding the image of the egg to the light, the chick can be seen inside reading the paper. Advertisement for *The Morning* newspaper, Nottingham, 1892.

Christmas time is "Carnival" time —

Mackintosh's
TOFFEE DE LUXE

ABOVE: Even before the ubiquitous box of Quality Street, Mackintosh were targeting the Christmas confectionary market. *Britannia & Eve*, 1929.

OPPOSITE: The name Hovis derives from the Latin 'Hominis Vis', meaning 'strength of man'. It was introduced in 1890 and by 1894 was advertised as supplied to the Queen. *Illustrated London News*, 1894.

Rival electric light bulb
advertisements.

ABOVE: Flattering theatrical
illumination, Mazda, *Britannia
& Eve*, 1929.

OPPOSITE: Powerful illumination
for the city, Osram, *Pan*, 1919.

Osram
G.E.C.
LAMPS
THE INITIALS G.E.C
ARE A GUARANTEE OF
BRITISH MANUFACTURE
OSRAM

ABOVE: McDougall's self-raising flour was trademarked in 1879, and is still in production today. Advertising envelope, 1880s.

LEFT: Trade card for J.M. Kronheim & Co., fine art chromo lithographers, 1880s.

OPPOSITE: Oil-fuelled bicycle lamps. The reverse of this sheet has a poem entitled the 'King of the Road', including the lines 'The "King" must be the lamp for me, as anyone may tell, I'll send for one from "Lucas", then I'm sure to look a swell'. Flyer, 1884.

PATENTED IN ENGLAND AND AMERICA.

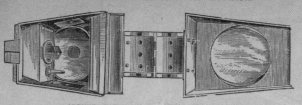

OPENED FOR PUTTING INTO THE WHEEL.

RETAIL PRICES.

CLOSED.

No. 1, Japanned, 12/6; Nickeled on tin, 17/6; Nickeled on brass, 23/–
No. 2,   ,,   14/–   ,,   20/–   ,,   26/–

For Tricycles, 2/– extra.

The nickel-plated on brass are highly finished, and very durable.

No. 1, with 3½-in. glass, for 52-in. wheels with 80 spokes, and No. 2, with 4-in.
glass, for 70 spoked wheels.

When opened, as shewn in the engraving, it can be easily slipped into the
wheel, and instantly secured on the axle by duplex spring clips. It has duplex
wick tubes, giving a large light, which is thrown far a-head of the machine by a
powerful German-silver reflector, making night riding perfectly safe and enjoyable.
*The axle leathers can be removed when worn out, and replaced by new ones by
sliding them round and out of the side plates*

"THE PIONEER," an ordinary sized lamp, with 3-in. front glass, on the same
patented principle as the "KING," is suited to wheels with about 100 spokes.

Japanned, 9/–; Nickel-plated, 14/–

"THE KING of the ROAD."

HEAD LAMP. No. 51.

With India Rubber spring, and shade for
throwing down the light.

No. 1, Japanned, 10/6; Nickeled on
tin, 15/–; Nickeled on brass, 21/–
No. 2, Japanned, 12/6; Nickeled on
tin, 17/6; Nickeled on brass, 23/–
No. 1 has 3½-in., and No. 2 has 4-in.
plate-glass front.

"THE CAPTAIN."

Registered No. 6360.

An excellent lamp, with newly registered
spring fastener for axle. Recommended
to all who want a good article at a low
price.

Japanned, 6/6; Nickel-plated, 10/6.

Burn Salad or Olive Oil. A good plan is to touch the Wick with
Paraffin, when it will ignite instantly the light is applied.

AGENT :

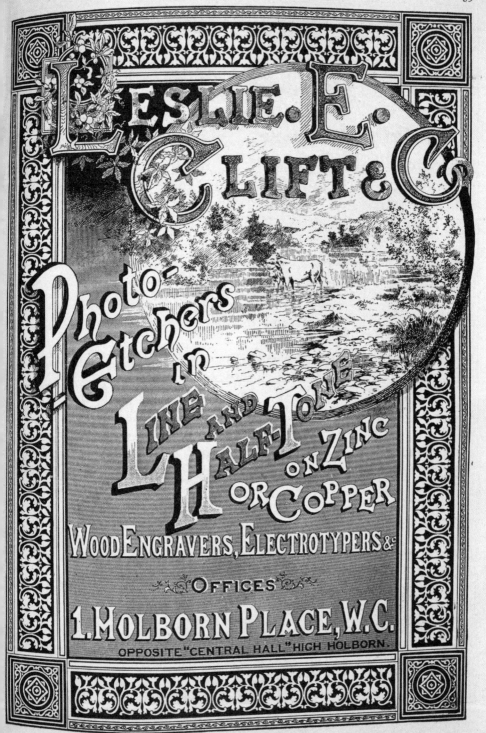

LESLIE. E. CLIFT & Co.

Photo-Etchers in Line and Half-Tone on Zinc or Copper

Wood Engravers, Electrotypers &

Offices

1. HOLBORN PLACE, W.C.

OPPOSITE "CENTRAL HALL" HIGH HOLBORN.

DE RYCKER & MENDEL
Fine ART Printers

ALL WE DO

WE DO WELL.

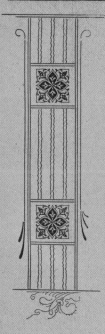

DOES POSTER
ADVERTISING PAY?

A great deal depends on the Poster. A good design is only half the battle, it must be properly treated by the printer to become

GOOD ADVERTISING.

"PICTORIAL PLACARDS,"

Our new booklet, with Reproductions in Colour of a few of our successful Posters, will give you our idea of it. Sent free to Advertisers upon application.

HART & LECLERCQ,

Sole Agents for the United Kingdom,

54, FLEET STREET, E.C.

OPPOSITE: Trade publications also started to flourish during the late 19th century, and were prime advertising spaces for specialist businesses. *The British Lithographer,* 1891.

ABOVE: Advertising advertising, within the pages of *Modern Advertising,* 1901.

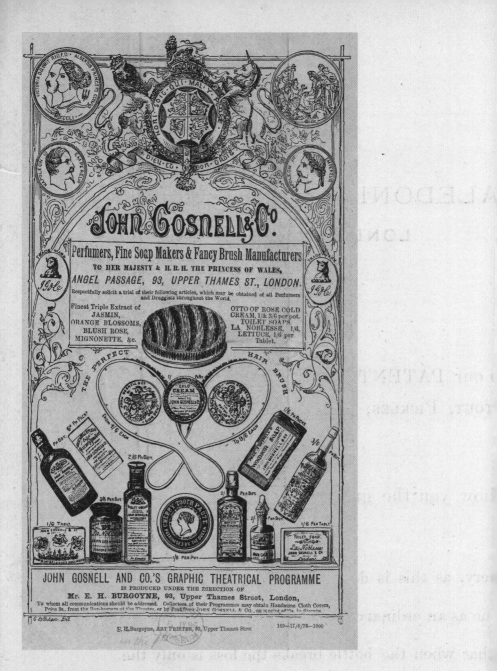

CHOC-FULL OF GOODNESS !

ABOVE: But of course chocolate
is good for you! Nestlé advert,
c. 1928.

SOLD BY THE LONDON AND LISBON CORK WOOD CO. LIMITED.

28 UPPER THAMES STREET LONDON.

VIRGIN FERN

Virgin Cork
the London & Lis
Co (limited) 28

FOR FERNERIES, GROTTOS, CASCADES, ARBOURS.

16/6 per Cwt.

"IT STICKS THE BILL AND STICKS THE BILL STICKER."

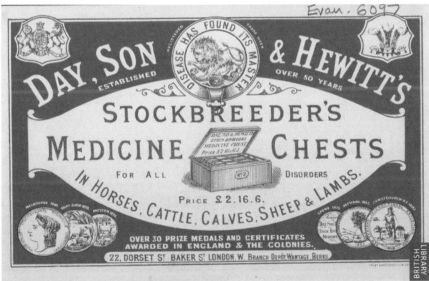

TOP: The reverse proclaims
Le Page's liquid glue to be the
'strongest adhesive known'.
Trade card, c. 1890.

ABOVE: The reverse of this sheet
gives descriptions of the medicines
to be carried in the chest, together
with testimonials. Flyer, c. 1882.

Imre Kiralfy's VENICE IN LONDON at Olympia.

Visitors may experience tha delightful sensation of gliding along tha beautiful aters of the rand Canal in e picturesque Gondolas of enice, manned by real Venetian Gondoliers.

TRUTH says:
"For the first time in a tolera- long time of shows and enter- nments I have been introduced a novelty that in my humble inion has not been half praised ough. . . . I defy anyone who rely gets his impression from wspapers or gossip to derive e very faintest idea of what is ntained in the huge Kensing-

ton building. . . . A black gondola awaits you, propelled by a stalwart Venetian in a striped guernsey of black and orange. Away you go on your voyage of discovery. Voices seem hushed, so extraordinary is the illusion. . . . On goes the gon- dola as in a dream: We stop at Salviati's and believe we are at Murano. They are making glass exactly as they do in the original establishment: There is the roar-

ing fiery furnace that would frighten Shadrach, Meshech, and Abednego. . . . After dinner you can stroll into the streets again, or smoke a cigar in the Rialto Gardens, but be sure and secure a seat for the theatrical entertainment, which is one of the strangest and most fascinating things of the kind I have ever beheld. The stage opening is about a quarter mile in extent,

and the water in front of it has an added mystery to the scene. . . . Hour after hour slips away and you do not appear to have been waiting for five minutes, so novel, varied, and fascinating is this mysterious and original show, which fairly eclipses the greatest recorded feats of Barnum and Sir Augustus Harris."

OPEN TWICE DAILY—12 to 5 and 6 to 11.

.0 and 6.0 for Promenade, Barcarolle Concerts, Modern Venice, Concerts, Gallery of the most celebrated Italian Pictures, &c. 30 and 8.30.—The Grand Spectacular Drama, "VENICE: the Bride of the Sea." Described by the *Times* as "by far the most important spectacle of its kind ever witnessed in London. . . . A triumph of stage-craft, greeted with unstinted applause." d after each performance Gondola Serenades in Modern Venice.

DMISSION : 1s., 2s., 3s., 4s., 5s., 6s. Boxes, £1. 1s. to £3. 3s.

Tickets of 3s. and upwards will be sold Two Weeks in advance.

ll these prices, from the lowest, include a Numbered and Reserved Seat for the Grand Spectacular Drama, admission to Modern Venice, the Promenade, Picture Galleries, &c. There are NO EXTRA CHARGES.

VERY SEAT IS NUMBERED AND RESERVED, SO THAT EVERY TICKET INSURES A SEAT. NO ADMISSION BEYOND SEATING CAPACITY OF HALL.

OW TO REACH VENICE IN LONDON AT OLYMPIA.

OLYMPIA can be approached from all Stations on all the leading Railways by booking to

ADDISON ROAD STATION

(OLYMPIA IS JUST OUTSIDE THIS STATION).

On all Stations on the District Railway book to Addison Road or West Kensington Station (West Kensington is within five minutes' walk from Olympia).

HUNDREDS OF OMNIBUSES PASS THE DOOR DAILY.

SPECIAL TRAINS TO MEET THE REQUIREMENTS OF VISITORS TO OLYMPIA

For particulars of which see the Companies' Handbills and other Announcements.

The STANDARD says : "A SUPERB ENTERTAINMENT!

PREVIOUS PAGES: 'Venice in London',
1892. The reverse of the advertising
leaflet on pages 118–119.

ABOVE: There is definitely a hint of
sybaritic luxury in this advert for the
Savoy Hotel, from the back page of
Savoy theatre programme, c. 1890.

OPPOSITE: Advertisement in the form
of an envelope for Overton's Oyster
Saloon & Restaurant, 1887.

BARRELLED OYSTERS TO ORDER.

OVERTON'S

OYSTER SALOON
&
RESTAURANT

WHISTABLE NATIVES

OPEN TILL 12.30 P.M. SEPERATE TABLES

FAMILIES SUPPLIED WITH FISH & ICE

NEW LUNCHEON, DINING AND SUPPER ROOMS

FISHMONGER POULTERER AND ICE MERCHANT.

LICENSED DEALER IN GAME.

COUNTRY ORDERS PUNCTUALLY ATTENDED TO

BY CONTRACT OR OTHERWISE

TELEPHONE 3164

BALCONY VIEW.

OPPOSITE VICTORIA STATION

3, 4, 5 & 6, VICTORIA BUILDINGS, S.W.

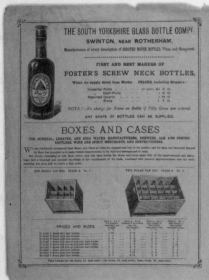
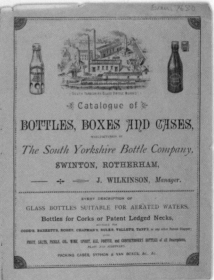

TOP: Glass bottles suitable for aerated waters, fruit, salts, pickle, oil and wine. Leaflet for South Yorkshire Bottle Company, 1885.

ABOVE: Confectionary bottles of all descriptions. Leaflet for South Yorkshire Bottle Company, 1885.

OPPOSITE: Cohen's Patent stoppered bottles. Advertising leaflet, 1881.

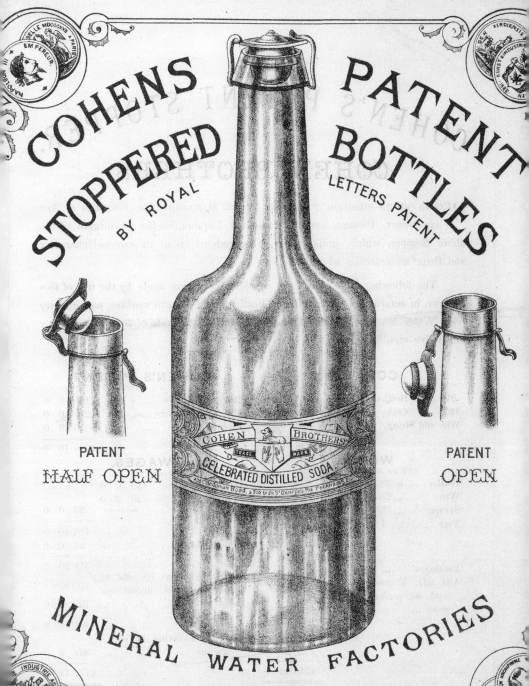

COHENS PATENT STOPPERED BOTTLES

BY ROYAL LETTERS PATENT

PATENT HALF OPEN

PATENT OPEN

COHEN BROTHERS

TRADE MARK

CELEBRATED DISTILLED SODA

438, Caledonian Road, & 205 to 211 St Georges Rd. Peckham, S.E.

MINERAL WATER FACTORIES

438, CALEDONIAN RD., LONDON, N.

AND

205, 206, 207, 208, 209, 210 & 211, St. Georges Rd. Peckham.

ALFRED J. ISAACS & SON, PRINTERS, 56, BISHOPSGATE ST. WITHIN.

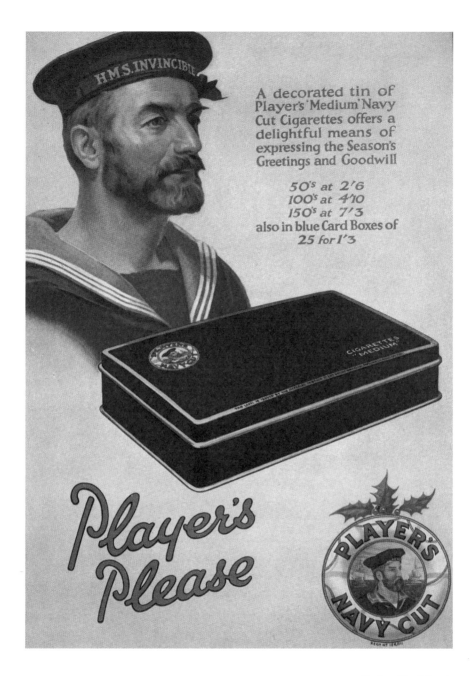

A decorated tin of Player's 'Medium' Navy Cut Cigarettes offers a delightful means of expressing the Season's Greetings and Goodwill

50's at 2'6
100's at 4'10
150's at 7'3
also in blue Card Boxes of
25 for 1'3

ABOVE: The slogan 'Player's Please' was an extremely successful piece of branding. In the 1920s and 1930s two thirds of all cigarettes sold in Britain were Player's. *Britannia & Eve*, 1929.

LEFT: 'The Finest the World Produces… Supplied in all first-class Hotels, Clubs and Stores throughout the World'. *The Times of India Annual*, 1919.

BOTTOM LEFT AND OVERLEAF: Paper bag proclaiming 'Harris's Sausages are the Best' on one side, and an illustration on the other of 'the winner of the Pork Sausage Derby', 1889.

TRADE

The Winner of the